Emotional Intelligence 2.0

How to Get Rid of Negative Thoughts

Zach Roger

Copyright © 2018 Zach Roger

All rights reserved.

© COPYRIGHT 2019 BY **ZACH ROGER** - ALL RIGHTS RESERVED.

In no way is it legal to reproduce, duplicate, or transmit any part of this document in either electronic means or in printed format. Recording of this publication is strictly prohibited and any storage of this document is not allowed unless with written permission from the publisher. All rights reserved.

The information provided herein is stated to be truthful and consistent, in that any liability, in terms of inattention or otherwise, by any usage or abuse of any policies, processes, or directions contained within is the solitary and utter responsibility of the recipient reader. Under no circumstances will any legal responsibility or blame be held against the publisher for any reparation, damages, or monetary loss due to the information herein, either directly or indirectly.
Respective authors own all copyrights not held by the publisher.

Legal Notice:
This book is copyright protected. This is only for personal use. You cannot amend, distribute, sell, use, quote or paraphrase any part of the content within this book without the consent of the author or copyright owner. Legal action will be pursued if this is breached.

Disclaimer Notice:
Please note the information contained within this document is for educational and entertainment purposes only. Every attempt has been made to provide accurate, up to date and complete, reliable information. No warranties of any kind are expressed or implied. Readers acknowledge that the author is not engaging in the rendering of legal, financial, medical or professional advice.

By reading this document, the reader agrees that under no circumstances are we responsible for any losses, direct or indirect, which are incurred as a result of the use of information contained within this document, including, but not limited to, —errors, omissions, or inaccuracies.

CONTENTS

	Introduction	1
1	Your personal litany of ills	3
2	Confronting your malicious subconscious	6
3	How I did it	11
4	Alert and attentive	16
	Conclusion	21

INTRODUCTION

Sometimes, we can be our own worst enemy.

Why have a nemesis who talks behind your back when you can do all the back-talking yourself, right?

And that's the problem with negative thinking. Many of us struggle with a toxic internal monologue that holds us back. We prevent ourselves from moving forward in life by repeating the same tired, self-flagellating negative statements to ourselves. And when we do this, we poison ourselves.

Emotional intelligence is a desirable trait, which allows us to gauge what's going on with those around us and to monitor our own internal landscape. That includes our internal monologue.

To be straight up with you, there's no point in modeling excellent emotional intelligence to those around us if we leave ourselves out of the fun.

So, this book is about a facet of emotional intelligence, which needs to be more thoroughly discussed – how to rid yourself of negative thoughts.

We're going to talk about the ground of emotional intelligence as your ability to regulate your emotions by being alive to them. But we're going a little further than that. We're going to teach you about how to motivate yourself despite your self-doubt and fear of moving forward (generated by that toxic internal monologue).

These are skills you can learn and, in doing so, you'll multiply the valuable quality of emotional intelligence that's so necessary for your success in life. As I've hinted above, approaching yourself with the same tools that you use to gauge other people's emotional status and to apply that information to situations at work and at home is the very root of developing EI to its highest potential. You need to start with yourself to successfully develop your emotional intelligence.

I thank your purchasing, downloading and reading this book. It's my hope that its contents will change the way you look at yourself, so you can change the way you interact with others and move forward in life successfully.

1 YOUR PERSONAL LITANY OF ILLS

A litany is a prayerful recitation. In its traditional, ecclesiastical form, the names of the saints are chanted, as their intercession is requested by the church congregation. But when it comes to negative thoughts, we all have a personal litany of ills.

This litany is very different. While the Litany of the Church asks the saints to deliver us from all manner of evil, the personal litany of ills goes something like this:

Because I'm so inadequate, I may as well not apply for that job.
I really suck at doing that.
Nobody likes me. Everybody hates me. I'm going to eat some worms.
I'm not attractive enough.
I'm not smart enough.
I'm a fraud.
Everyone knows I'm a fraud. They're just too nice to say so.

These are just a few examples of the personal litany of ills, which has become your toxic internal monologue over time. Where do these thoughts come from?

While negative thoughts are self-generated, they have their origins outside of us. The things people say (especially our parents). Personal failures (which are usually minor but which have stuck with us). Negative experiences with other people. Our personal litany of ills can grow rapidly to become a corrosive canon of beliefs we hold about ourselves which are not true.

Or, perhaps, there's a small grain of truth of which we've created a palace of negativity.

Either way, these thoughts hold us back, preventing us from reaching our full potential and being the light in the world we're all capable of being.

Understanding the litany

You weren't born with negative thoughts about yourself. They came from somewhere in your environment.

Parents, teachers, friends, acquaintances, even strangers can set us on a path of negative thinking. While we may not remember the words that triggered the negative thought, our subconscious mind remembers the import of those words.

Thinking of your mind as a palace in which the great room is your conscious mind and the crypt is your subconscious mind is helpful. While the subconscious is deep within your mind's palace, it's often a powerful driver of negative thinking. At any moment, it can assert itself. All it takes is a stray word, or an unexpected interaction and the import of the words, which gave birth to a negative thought resurfaces. You're "triggered" and a flood of negative thinking overwhelms your mind.

The great hall (conscious thinking) is where your ability to reason and to thinking logically reside. This is also where the controls are to your body and its actions. Negative thoughts also hang out in the great room of your mind.

In the crypt (subconscious mind), the controls for involuntary actions like breathing and other systems of the body you rarely think about reside. This is where the "riding a bike" responses live. Once you learn to ride a bicycle, you never forget. It becomes second nature and you what to do to propel the bike and remain upright doesn't even cross your mind. You just get on and ride.

But it's in the crypt that the secret life of your mind lurks, waiting to undermine you with incidents in your life, which have led to your personal litany of ills.

Getting a handle on your mind's secret life is the key to eliminating negative thinking.

Knowing the difference

The first step toward freeing yourself from the toxic influence of negative thinking is the ability to discern the difference between thoughts, which are constructive and build you up and thoughts, which are destructive and tear you down.

At the root of negative thinking are old assertions others have made about you and experiences, which have served to personally indict you (with your full complicity). When these arise as negative thoughts, it's crucial that you understand that what's driving your conscious mind into the crypt is fear.

And there is nothing more negative and threatening than fear.

What you need to know is how that fear is being produced by thoughts and experiences from your past. That means delving into the crypt of your palace for the source of the negative thinking that's doing nothing more valuable than derailing your life's potential.

Cleaning out the crypt

When a negative thought begins to form in your mind, it's accompanied by an emotion. One of those is fear. Another is sadness. But a negative thought is always accompanied by a negative emotion. This toxic feedback loop of negative thinking not only holds you back in life. It can affect your health when it becomes a habit.

So, when these thoughts arise, it's important that you identify, label and above all, challenge them.

This is the work of your conscious mind. Being alive to the negative thought you're having allows you to grab hold of it, examine and challenge it and eliminate it. That's what cleaning out the crypt is all about. It's a long-term project of profound self-examination and improvement.

In our next chapter, we'll be talking about practical ways to clean out your crypt, using tools to help you along the way. Let's get ready to clear out the cobwebs in your crypt and by so doing, stop your personal litany of ills in its tracks, so you can get on with your life.

2 CONFRONTING YOUR MALICIOUS SUBCONSCIOUS

Your attitude toward yourself as a person impacts everything around you. If you believe yourself to be unworthy and incompetent, others pick up on that. You exude the negativity of your beliefs and self-image. So, believing that the world and everyone in it is against you is a bit of a self-fulfilling prophecy. You allow that thought to control you and others notice.

Your beliefs about yourself are rooted in the subconscious mind lurking in the palace crypt.

What you choose to absorb as "real" in terms of the way you think about yourself and your value as a human being is your reality. When you allow your negative thoughts to take the wheel, you are turning those thoughts into immutable beliefs, which are hurting and hindering you.

These beliefs can seem very real. They can seem as though they've been proven beyond the shadow of a reasonable doubt. But the truth is that your personal litany of ills is not real at all. That litany is based on events, which have long passed, other people's invalid and insensitive opinions and statements and your tacit acceptance of them.

I know that because I've had to confront my malicious subconscious in order to tame it and to live the positive reality that is my life. We'll discuss my personal journey a little later. For now, though, let's get down to clearing out the cobwebs in your crypt.

So what?

Negative thoughts almost always cycle through your head as the result of being triggered by incidents and words, which somehow mimic that origin story of those thoughts.

For example, if a teacher in grade school once said you were lazy, similar assertions in your present life can bring that statement back up, galvanizing and validating it.

Your response to the negative thought is: "So what?"

So what if that teacher said that about you? You know it's not true and you have numerous reasons to know that's the case. You know you're not lazy because you throw yourself into what you do for a living, your family and your passions. What's important here is to create a means for reminding yourself that you're not lazy when the negative thought and the corresponding words/incident are triggered.

When the thought arises, just say it. Just say, "So what?" Say it loud. Say it proud.

Then tell yourself why you know you're not lazy and why that teacher was being abusive and unnecessarily cruel. Put the blame for the negative thought on the shoulders of its long-ago progenitor, and leave it there.

Changing the negative thought is work, but it is well worth doing. Your conscious mind needs to override the contents of your subconscious mind to overcome the thought and thus, the self-hating belief.

What you're doing is rejecting the negative thought, which has led to a belief becoming rooted in you. It's in that rejection that you become the master of your own mind, instead of being its unwitting, self-loathing puppet.

The "So what?" may look like a question but what it is, in truth, is an affirmation and validation of the truth you know about yourself. Replacing that negative thought with the knowledge (a conscious act) that you are not that at all is how you move forward and shed negativity as a way of life.

Then again…

At this point, we should remember that sometimes we allow a negative thought to hold us back from changing something about ourselves we don't like.

For example, the belief that you're lazy can become a truth about you. You can absorb that long-ago statement to the degree that you actualize it. If that's the case, the negative thought can be transformative.

The belief that you're lazy may have become a self-fulfilling prophecy and you may have embraced it as an easy way out. That's how you undermine your own efforts and your own life.

Transforming that negative belief calls for some introspection. Looking inside yourself and asking whether you haven't made that false belief settled law (in which you decide it's how you're going to live because you can't do anything about it – because you're too lazy) could change the way you deal with the belief and its destructive presence in your life.

A bit like turning lemons into lemonade, transforming negative thinking into a self-directed project to improve the way you live thoroughly conquers the negativity by turning it into the truth – a positive belief about yourself.

Being honest by recognizing the fact that you've accepted the belief as an excuse to underachieve and live a less-than-fulfilling life is your ticket to freedom. You wrestle the thought to the ground and hit it over the head with a rock. Then, you actively work to change what the belief has wrought in your character.

A clear message

To successfully kill negative beliefs about yourself, it's essential that you be clear in the message you're sending your subconscious. There are no half measures here. There's only a full-throated rejection of the negative belief that's eroding your confidence and self-esteem.

This is where an intentional frame of mind enters the picture. If you're going to clean out the cobwebs in your palace's crypt, you want them all gone. All of them and the nasty spiders who made them. You want that place to be immaculate and re-engineered to support your growing self-confidence.

If you're taking on the fact that you have so internalized the belief that you're lazy, then you can't tell yourself, "I need to stop believing this about myself, but maybe it's too late. Maybe I'm just too lazy to change!"

How useless an approach is that?

To clarify your message, meet any rupture in your resolve with the opposite of your negative thought, as follows:

I am lazy.

I am not lazy. I'm hardworking.

Or, if you've succumbed to the belief and have given it dominion over your life:

I am lazy.

I will transform that laziness into positive action. I will move towards my goals.

It's only when those conscious and unconscious thoughts match - when you've replaced negativity with positivity - that you'll see profound change.

At our cores

At our cores is a set of beliefs about ourselves, which guide us through life.

The negative thinker has unwholesome, negative beliefs about his or her character and worth as a human being. These are formed early on life and derive from the comments and behavior of other people. Our part of the equation is acceptance. And when we're young, we don't have the ability to reason ourselves out of that acceptance and so, we internalize these comments and behaviors as the truth about who we are. We're also very vulnerable to the opinions and attitudes of other people because we so desperately want to be liked and accepted. In that vulnerability is the genesis of negative thinking.

To be able to function as a fully-realized human being, our core beliefs must be positive. Why should anyone else believe in us if we don't believe in ourselves?

Self-affirmations like:
I'm a good person.
People like me.
I work hard.
My work is good.
I'm honest.

These are positive self-beliefs that others can sense in us. If we don't think of ourselves in constructive ways, other people can tell (almost instinctively) that our orientation is negative. That's not attractive. It doesn't inspire confidence or respect.

And it's when we're at our most emotionally vulnerable that the negative beliefs we have about ourselves come to the fore, drowning out the positive. When we're upset, angry or have suffered a personal loss of some kind, a little crack forms in our internal defenses and those negative thoughts and beliefs take over.

The core beliefs we hold true, having been formed prior to becoming adults, are not written in stone. They're written on the delicate psyches of children, well before the age of reason. Having achieved the age of reason, adults are equipped to take an inventory of their negative beliefs about themselves and track their origins.

In doing so, it becomes increasingly clear that some of our most compelling self-perceptions were planted there with errant words. These were not things we thought about ourselves. These were things others said about us.

Along the way, those childhood incidents take root and became our realities. But taking inventory by unpacking your most negative thoughts and systematically rejecting them, recognizes them as unhealthy and unworthy of your attention.

Remember that any belief you have about yourself has no value to you if it doesn't build you up as a person. So, getting to the heart of the matter (where the belief/thought came from) helps you understand that external factors led you to the thought/belief, skewing your self-perception.

And external input, which is thoughtless, careless and false, has no place in your subconscious. It's flotsam. It's ambient junk. It's covered in cobwebs, which must be cleared away.

And the quickest way to do that is to create an inventory of your recurring negative thoughts, identify the source and create a corresponding affirmation.

I'm not going to lie. This is a serious introspective project. By doing it, you'll get to know the truth about yourself. You'll come to know whether the negative thought has become embedded to the point it's a self-fulfilling prophecy. By drilling down into your subconscious crypt with your adult ability to reason and extrapolate information, which is empirical and sound, you can either eliminate or transform the negative thought/belief.

In the next chapter, I'd like to tell you about my own experience of overcoming negative thinking and how it's changed my life immeasurably. I want you to know that you're not alone; that we all struggle with the reality of negative thinking and how powerful an influence it can be in our lives. In that reality is liberation and solidarity, so let me share with you a little of my own experience.

3 HOW I DID IT

Those of us who've struggled with negative thinking have similar stories. One minute we were innocent children, exploring the world with endless energy, curiosity and delight. The next, we were neurotic basket cases, believing with every fiber of our beings that we weren't quite good enough.

So, what happened? I don't know what happened to any of you, but maybe some of what happened to me will sound familiar. It's often the case that hearing one isn't alone is good news, so I'm sharing a bit about my own negative thinking and how eliminating it from my life grew my emotional intelligence by growing my own self-awareness and self-love. The positive frame of mind I wake up with every day is what made that happen, but it demanded a personal journey of introspection and learning how to still the negativity once and for all.

That "ouch" moment

You know as well as I do that there's probably a specific "ouch" moment you go back to for your negative reinforcement. This was a seminal moment in your career as a negative thinker. It was the moment in which your very value as a human being was called into question, propelling you into an adulthood of self-doubt and fear of failure.

For me, that "ouch" moment has lost its sting, but for years, it would be the siren song that routinely turned my mind away from the achievements I should have boldly pursued and toward my personal perceived inadequacies.

I was in elementary school at the time in maybe Grade 4. I was smart and over-achieving. As precocious and exploratory as they come, I knew I was headed for the big time. I didn't know what that might be, but I was already thinking of careers like law. My world had no ceiling.

And then, I was confronted by a teacher who wanted to "help" me by detaining me every day after school to work on my lisp.

My lisp, at the time, was pronounced and slightly embarrassing but the other kids didn't tease me about it much. It was just part of who I was. But this teacher decided that I could not have a lisp; that I needed to learn how to "properly" pronounce "s" sounds. But the longer this went on, the more frustrated I became. I couldn't make that sound like most people and frankly, I hadn't even thought too much about it until that first day when this teacher so helpfully brought to my attention that I was "doing it wrong."

Finally, I refused to attend these sessions any longer, with the full support of my parents. Of course, I had to go home at the point of tears for that to happen.

While his intentions may have been noble, the damage done by the episode stuck with me for years. I loved singing but was afraid to try. I loved being in the drama club but feared opening my mouth in front of an audience. I struggled to answer questions in class, looking for ways to avoid the letter "s" at all costs. I would carefully construct my sentences to avoid it as much as humanly possible.

There were many other "ouchy" moments in my life, to be sure, but the "lisp episode" was by far the most impactful. It was to wound me for many years, as I struggled to be who I knew I could be, afraid to open my mouth the whole time.

And that won't get you far in life.

Recognizing the wound

It wasn't until I was on the cusp of my 30s that a friend mentioned a trait he'd noticed in me. He said, "You always choose the storm cloud over the silver lining."

I was a little taken aback, but when I asked him what he meant, he explained that while I usually seemed happy and positive, he knew that wasn't the case. Whenever an opportunity to change my life would come up, I'd make excuses. I'd weave a tale of worst-case scenarios, which would probably arise the moment I reached out for the opportunity.

I thought about it. I thought about what my friend had said to me, reeling it out in my mind and checking it for holes. But I knew he was right and the more I thought about it, the more I thought about the "lisp episode." The more I realized that this was the wound in myself I needed to reconcile in order to move forward.

Was I still laboring under a misguided teacher's attempt to fix me? Was I still treating that episode as though I needed to be fixed? Was I still in 4th Grade?

I supposed I was. I supposed that my potential had been voluntarily frozen in time. I say voluntarily because I was moving into my 30s. My 4th Grade self couldn't have been expected to have the psychological muscle to wrestle that "ouch" moment to the ground. But surely, my adult self was up to it?

I decided that, yes. I was up to it. And that's when my life began to change.

Self-compassion

We tend to think of compassion as a human effort that flows outward. "Feeling with" other people is a noble quality and one which makes the world a better place to live.

But how can you model compassion for others when you have none for yourself?

Self-compassion is about healing the wound your "ouch" moment created. As I've said, we've all had more than one "ouch" moment, but they tend to throw the original wound into relief, making it more menacingly 3-dimensional. It's that original wound which seeks the validation of more negativity. It attracts it like a magnet.

The wounded, negative thinker seeks more negativity in order to validate the beliefs they've accumulated about themselves. Instead of rejecting the original wound, they pile on the scar tissue every time a stray word or action comes their way.

Every romantic involvement that fails. Every friendship that ends. Every employment rejection, firing and incident of professional discipline. Every jerk that cuts you off in traffic. Every coffee order the barista gets wrong.

It all adds up to one big, negative ball of angst that you do your best to keep at bay by putting on a happy face, all the while believing yourself to be inadequate and unworthy.

But what I learned on my journey away from negative thinking is that self-compassion is the balm your wound needs to heal.

Who am I?

Your starting point in the project of putting a lid on the negative thinking and beliefs which are derailing your life is to answer the question, "Who am I?"

Creating an inventory of positive personal achievements and attributes is a powerful weapon against the self-destructive tendency to view yourself in a negative light. You will need a pad of paper and a pen or pencil.

Think about all the things you've done in your life that you're proud of.

These can be anything from turning up for work on time, all the time, to passing your driver's test. Allow your mind to go to the moments that lifted you up and made you feel you were worthwhile, after all.

Now, write down your most positive traits. Are you neat? Write it down. Are you a good worker? Are you reliable? Are you honest? All these things are positive traits and they count because what you write about yourself is your truth, when you focus on what you like about who you are.

Here's the thing – my 4th Grade self didn't care about my lisp until someone told that poor kid that it was unacceptable by trying to fix it. I can give that teacher the benefit of the doubt or I can think he had some weird problem with people who lisp. In the end, it doesn't matter. What matters is my own conception of what it means to have a lisp. And giving that teacher the benefit of the doubt is the right thing to do because it heals the resentment.

It neutralizes the wound's source as being just as fragile, human and fallible as I am.

I still lisp. I don't care, though. I accept the way I speak and most others do, too. The occasional person who points it out tends to be a socially inept clod, which is their problem – not mine. I've never attended speech therapy, either because I now think of my lisp as just another fabulous, funky part of who I am.

And that was possible because I healed the wound with self-compassion. To do that, I didn't just need to sit down that one time to write out positive things about myself. I had to actively remind myself, every day, that I was exactly where I was supposed to be in that moment because I was worthy.

And where I was excited me. I was on the edge of finding out just how far I could go because I'd finally healed that "ouch" moment. So, I continued with my positive affirmations about who I genuinely am, every day. I started a journal.

And it's your journal that's going to be your best friend, as you move toward giving yourself the same compassion you usually reserve for other people.

A daily project

I tend to think of journaling as an activity for the evenings when the day is almost done and you're just about ready to turn in. I sit in a comfortable place, empty my mind of extraneous thoughts and simply jot down the high points of my day.

Once I'm through the high points, I note the low points. They usually pale in comparison to the truly great moments.

After I've gone through the chronological review of my day, I identify moments in which my positive attributes and abilities were in play and how they made the day even better.

In short, I blow my own horn.

And if your "ouch" moment is someone telling you not to be so crazy about yourself, then knowing fully that you have good reason to be is the antidote.

I'm not telling you to be a narcissist (those people aren't at all well). I'm telling you to appreciate and love yourself as the worthy person you are. You have something in you that the world needs. If you're a negative thinker (as I once was), then you need to leave that "ouch" moment and all the scar tissue that original wound has accumulated behind. You need to replace it with the knowledge of what your value and contribution can become.

Reviewing your day every evening keeps you honest and away from the negative thinking that's been holding you back. Making note of how your aptitudes and talents changed the course of the day or made it better (in even the smallest way) is a self-esteem builder that helps you re-tool your frame of mind. Killing negativity with a positive way of seeing yourself and what you bring to the party is an effective support, when done each day, intentionally.

And intention is extremely important in this model. You need to mean it. You need to believe it and you need to do it. You need to know in your heart that you want to excuse the negativity from your mind and your life.

So, blow your own horn as I did and continue to do. Believe in yourself and stop believing the old stories, which have roosted in your head because of something that happened too long ago to care about. You are free to be who you truly are, unimpeded by the thoughtless intervention or negative aspersions of others.

Next, let's explore how turning off negative thinking makes room for emotional intelligence that's been informed by your own journey.

4 ALERT AND ATTENTIVE

"Ask yourself, is there negativity in me at this moment? Then, become alert and attentive to your thoughts as well as your emotions."
Eckhart Tolle

Eckhart Tolle's simple prescription in the quote shown above is all about self-regulation. Without self-regulation, your emotions rule you. You lose control and you also lose the social capital you need to succeed.

Your thoughts and emotions work closely together, creating the framework for the moment you're living in, right now. When your thoughts are negative, it's likely that your emotions will follow suit and that toxic feedback will never close unless you do the important work of self-regulation.

This isn't a "pie in the sky" type of discussion, folks. The idea that you're able to self-regulate your thoughts and emotions is a scientifically proven reality. In truth, if you can self-regulate, you can "re-wire" your neural pathways to permanently gain control of the quality of your thinking and of the attending emotions.

Executive control training

Published in the journal NeuroImage, a January 2016 study conducted at the Ben-Gurion University of the Negev in Israel monitored the brain activity of a group of 26 volunteers.

The study used executive control training to affect the way study participants responded to negative stimuli. Executive control training correlates to the Buddhist practice of mindfulness, which allows the brain to detach from negative or unpleasant stimuli. This sense of detachment amounts to intellectual and emotional regulation.

Some participants in the Ben-Gurion study followed a more intense type of training. During the study, the amygdala (associated with negative emotions like anxiety and sadness) showed drastically reduced activity when confronted by the study's examples of negativity. In addition, the amygdala was seen to be more effectively connected to the part of the frontal cortex implicated in emotional regulation.

The study's findings have numerous real-world applications, including the treatment of clinically depressed people and those struggling with PTSD (Post-Traumatic Stress Disorder).

But what's genuinely astounding about this study and its findings is that it undergirds the idea that the brain is plastic organ (subject to change). The structures and connections of the brain and how they work can be reinvented by training people to self-regulate and to choose not to attach to negative thoughts and the emotions that come with them.

In other words, you can re train your brain to think positively and optimistically instead of negatively and pessimistically. This re-training needn't even be formal. My own efforts prove that and soon, yours will too.

Think first

Negative thinkers tend to pre-judge every situation as being inherently threatening or unfavorable. They further allow their thinking to adhere to their emotions, which they then reveal inappropriately and sometimes, self-destructively.

Acting on impulse is a tremendous problem for many people. This begins in childhood and unless a child is actively taught self-regulation and mindfulness about how others perceive impulsive behavior, it can endure into adulthood.

But as adults, shouldn't we be held accountable for our conduct? Shouldn't we be able to stop, think and prevent emotional outbursts, which not only cast us in a bad light but harm those around us?

Of course, we should. Some of us just need to work a little harder at it than others.

Adults who lose their cool under pressure aren't going to be considered for the top-flight positions, which demand the ability to, self-regulate. In fact, self-regulation is one of the most important components of emotional intelligence. Starting with our self-awareness and ability to detect and halt the formation of negative thoughts and emotions, we enhance our ability to detect the emotional states of others. Self-awareness and self-regulation lead to a heightened awareness of where those around us are, emotionally and help us to address the meaning and potential consequences of their emotions.

Mind yourself

Mindfulness is the ability to live in the moment as it is. Without embellishment, mindfulness allows us to see the truth in every moment we live and in so doing, the truth others are living concurrently.

Mindfulness can be encouraged with tools like deep breathing, journaling (as we've discussed) and taking a moment to think before responding to any given statement or situation. All these tools force our brains to relax, instead of seeking the instant gratification being demanded by our negative thinking and emotions. At the core of mindfulness is being alert to your internal monologue and actively seeking to regulate and reform it.

Reappraising

Pragmatism is the ability to process information that competes with your appraisal of any given situation and absorb it. By stepping back from your personal viewpoint and taking a 360-degree tour of factors you may not have taken note of, you're better equipped to navigate it appropriately, without negativity knocking it all sideways.

A big part of the ability to reappraise situations and scenarios is to give others the benefit of the doubt. For example, it's possible that the co-worker you believe disrespected you by not acknowledging your contribution to a project didn't know what your contribution was. That guy on the bus who banged into you may have a balance issue that caused the collision. Your dry cleaning isn't ready because there was a technical issue.

In other words, it's not all about you. The world is not out to get you. There are factors involved which make the situation, scenario or incident innocuous and these factors are what transform the complexion of what you've misinterpreted as a personal comment on you.

No, Virginia. It's really not all about you!

Instead of having a confrontation, or building up resentment against others, a reappraisal allows you to step back and see things as they really are before allowing yourself to spiral into a negative frenzy of self-loathing and recriminations against yourself and others.

How does self-regulation change you?

Being able to effectively self-regulate changes everything. Once you've become more skilled at it, you'll stop thinking everyone's against you or dislikes you and start seeing them as the benign entities they are.

You'll see the challenges that come up in life, work and love as opportunities to grow. You'll be a better communicator who doesn't sit on resentments but gets to the heart of the matter by talking about whatever's happened to the person or people it happened with.

When you're able to mindfully regulate your toxic internal monologue and reform it to become something positive and optimistic, you'll find that you're clear about your goals and will act according to your self-professed values and morals.

And even if you don't believe it will benefit you in any significant way, you do your best. You don't do a half-assed job because you must. You do a great job because you want to and because you can.

Best of all you, your mindfulness will lead to greater contentment and satisfaction. When you stop your toxic internal monologue, you start the nurturing internal monologue, which leads to inner calm and the ability to overcome the bad times (because you know that good times are right behind them).

The element of choice

Everything in this book is leading to one conclusion – that you have a choice. You have a choice to think the negative thoughts you allow to rule you. And you have a choice to allow your negative emotions to rule you. Choosing a better way forward is why you're here.

You and you alone are responsible for your own words, reactions and thoughts. While you may feel that life has been tough on you and that you're at a disadvantage, that's your choice too. You can choose to reject this kind of self-undermining mindset, exchanging it for one, which will propel you forward.

When you feel the negativity in you rising, know that you define the outcome. You say whether that negativity gets to come out to play. Self-awareness and alertness to the thoughts that crowd your head at difficult moments leads to understanding that these moments are minor players in the great sweep of your life story. But those same difficult moments can be self-fulfilling prophets of doom when you fail to regulate yourself and let the dark cloud over your head win the day.

In choosing to be the master of your thoughts and emotions, you're choosing to live a more fruitful life. Negative thinking and the emotions that come with it may have become your daily reality. Maybe you think you're stuck with it.

But that's a choice too. And it's a negative choice.

You have within you the ability to overcome negative thinking to move into a brighter future. Change is not easy. No one ever said it was. But I know it's possible because I've lived it. I've learned to detect moments, which have the potential to resurrect my inner demons. Detaching from them, hearing what's really being said and seeing things as they are (and not as I'd formerly conditioned myself to believe they were) is the royal road to using my limited energy for more fruitful, positive pursuits.

If I can manage it, I know darned well you can, too.

I'm grateful that you've downloaded this book and that you've read this far. I know that you're as able as anyone else to reform your negative thinking patterns in favor of an emotionally intelligent approach to life that builds up instead of tearing down. All you need to do is make the decision to proceed.

And if you've read this far, I know that decision has been made.

CONCLUSION

Negativity thinking is one of the most corrosive habits people can get into. It damages relationships at home and at work. It damages self-esteem and it hinders career progress.

But so many of us engage in it as a way of life. The cobwebbed crypt cries out for recognition and we respond by allowing it to invade the great room of our palace. And you've grown weary of it, which is why you're here. You ardently desire change and I trust that the contents of this book have given you an idea as to how you might go about it.

Having been a victim of my own negative thinking, I'm aware of just how destructive it can be. So, doing something for yourself to change its toxic presence in your life by evicting it from your mind is a positive step forward. It's a step you've already taken just by choosing to read this book.

But you have many more steps to take to get into the valuable habit of self-regulation and the ability to see things are they really are and not as you've become conditioned to seeing them.

There is world out there waiting for what you have to offer. Your gifts and aptitudes are unique and they're desperately needed. But to offer them wholeheartedly, your belief in yourself and your way of seeing the world must change.

Taming your personal litany of ills and your malicious sub-conscious are at the heart of being able to gift yourself with the same compassion you show others. You deserve it, too. You deserve a life, which has been freed of the toxicity of negative thinking. Self-regulating effectively and being pragmatic about what happens out there in the world are important skills that the most sought-after talent is in command of.

And soon, you will be too.

Trust in the future. Believe in yourself. Give others the benefit of the doubt. Know that you're just one more fragile human life on the planet but a life with much to offer a world in need of optimism and positivity. Leaving negativity behind, you're choosing to strike out for the higher ground you know you can get to.

You've got this!

www.ingramcontent.com/pod-product-compliance
Lightning Source LLC
Chambersburg PA
CBHW071256070526
44583CB00017B/2498